ENGLAND

People began coming to England thousands of years ago. The Romans came, then the Angles and Saxons, then the Vikings, and later the French. Now, in the twenty-first century, people from all over the world live here in England.

And people still come to England – millions of visitors every year. Visitors who want to know more about the country that is England. There is London of course, but there is so much more . . .

So come with us and visit England – its cities and countryside, north and south, east and west. Learn about interesting places to visit – castles and gardens, churches and theme parks. There are many things to see – boat races, football, cricket, and theatre. And find out about English clothes, shopping, food, and some of the best music in the world.

OXFORD BOOKWORMS LIBRARY
Factfiles

England

Stage 1 (400 headwords)

Factfiles Series Editor: Christine Lindop

JOHN ESCOTT

England

OXFORD UNIVERSITY PRESS

OXFORD
UNIVERSITY PRESS

Great Clarendon Street, Oxford OX2 6DP

Oxford University Press is a department of the University of Oxford.
It furthers the University's objective of excellence in research, scholarship,
and education by publishing worldwide in

Oxford New York

Auckland Cape Town Dar es Salaam Hong Kong Karachi
Kuala Lumpur Madrid Melbourne Mexico City Nairobi
New Delhi Shanghai Taipei Toronto

With offices in

Argentina Austria Brazil Chile Czech Republic France Greece
Guatemala Hungary Italy Japan Poland Portugal Singapore
South Korea Switzerland Thailand Turkey Ukraine Vietnam

oxford and oxford english are registered trade marks of
Oxford University Press in the UK and in certain other countries

ISBN: 978 0 19 423380 4

A complete recording of this Bookworms edition of
England is available.

Printed in China

Word count (main text): 4,640

For more information on the Oxford Bookworms Library,
visit www.oup.com/elt/gradedreaders

Illustration page 2 by Gareth Riddiford

The publishers would like to thank the following for their kind permission to reproduce photographs:
Alamy Images pp10 (Trafford Centre, Manchester/Tony Smith), 11 (Lowry Gallery, Salford Quays/Ange), 12
(Millennium Bridge, Newcastle/Mike Kipling Photography), 14 (Bridge of Sighs/Steve Vidler), 16 (Clifton
Suspension Bridge/Eric Nathan), 18 (Bamburgh Castle, Northumberland/Richard Burdon), 19 (Yorkshire Dales/
Mike Kipling Photography), 20 (Norfolk Broads/EYESITE), 21 (New Forest ponies, Hampshire/Steve Vidler), 23
(bedroom in the Royal Pavilion, Brighton/Heritage Image Partnership Ltd), 26 (Spinball Wizard ride, Alton
Towers/Ruby), 27 (The Minack Theater, Penzance/Roger Cracknell 01/classic), 29 (Glastonbury Festival/Tom
Corban), 30 (rugby match/Graham Wilson), 31 (cricket match/John Potter), 32 (English breakfast/Neil Rouse),
33 (English afternoon tea/kevin nicholson), 34 (Lancashire Hotpot/travellinglight), 34 (fish and chips/Michael
Kemp), 36 (London Fashion Week/London Entertainment), 37 (Brighton shops/Ian Shaw), 39 (Notting Hill
Carnival, London/Brendan Bell), 40 (Cowes Week yachting/Peter Titmuss), 44 (cricket match, Surrey/Peter
Phipp/Travelshots.com), 49 (Salford Quays, The Lowry/julie woodhouse); Getty Images pp1 (Cotswold village/
Rachel Husband), 1 (West Dorset/Dave Young / Design Pics), 1 (performance at The Globe Theatre/Oli Scarff),
3 (Hadrian's Wall/paul mcgreevy), 5 (Brick Lane, London/Doug McKinlay), 6 (Buckingham Palace guards/
Stuart Black), 7 (George Benson performing/Steve Thorne), 8 (Grand National/Mike Hewitt), 13 (York Minster/
Neale Clark), 17 (Lake District in Autumn/Derek Croucher), 25 (Kew Gardens, England/Latitudestock), 35
(Punk fashion/Alex Segre), 38 (University boat race/Richard Heathcote); Stephen Hawkins pp22-23 (Blenheim
Palace); OUP pp24 (Stonehenge/Digital Vision), 44 (boat on river/Mike Stone), 44 (roast beef/Stockbyte), 44
(Bodiam Castle/Corel), 49 (surfers on beach/Blend Images), 49 (Crumock Water/Corel); Shutterstock pp4
(detail of the Bayeux Tapestry/jorisvo), 9 (Royal Liver Building at night/Paul Reid), 15 (Roman Baths, Bath/
antb), 44 (Hamlet performed in Russia/ID1974), 44 (Sandbanks Beach, Dorset/ian woolcock).

CONTENTS

Castle Combe, an
English village

1   Beautiful England

About twenty-five million people visit England every year. They come from countries all over the world. Nearly all of them go to London first, and some never go out of that great city.

London is a wonderful place, but there are many more exciting and interesting places across the country. Many of these places can tell you more about England and the English people.

There are green hills, quiet little villages, long beaches, beautiful old churches, and English gardens. And there are exciting big cities with great food, shops, and music.

You can see a Shakespeare play, or listen to great music twenty-four hours a day with thousands of other people. You can watch a game of cricket or football, take a boat along one of the rivers, or visit an old castle.

Yes, England is a very beautiful country. But who are the English . . . ?

Abbotsbury Hill

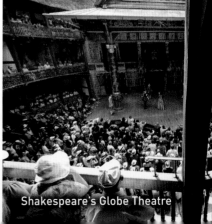

Shakespeare's Globe Theatre

Scotland

Newcastle-upon-Tyne •

Northumbria

Lake District

Isle of Man

Yorkshire

York •

Manchester •   Sheffield •

Liverpool •

England

Birmingham •

Norfolk

Norwich •

Cambridge •

Wales

Oxford •

London •

Bristol •
• Bath

Hampshire

Brighton •

Dorset

Bournemouth •

Cornwall

Isle of Wight

Newquay •

0   100 km

N

Norway

Denmark

Ireland   United
          Kingdom

Germany

France

0   900 km

2 Who are the English?

The name 'England' comes from 'Angle-land'. The Angle and Saxon people came here from Europe in the fifth and sixth centuries, and they called it Angle-land.

Before them, the Romans lived here for about four hundred years. They made houses and roads. And they made a town next to the River Thames, and called it Londinium. Today its name is London.

The Angles and Saxons came across the North Sea from north-west Germany and southern Denmark. Later the Vikings came from Denmark and Norway.

The Romans built Hadrian's Wall

In 1066, England had a new king. He was William of Normandy, the famous William the Conqueror. When he came to England, many French people came with him.

In the nineteenth century, thousands of Irish people came to England and stayed here, and many Jewish families came from Eastern Europe and Russia.

All through the twentieth century, people came to England and made a new life here. After the Second World War, many came from the West Indies, Africa, and Asia. In the 1980s, people from Vietnam came because they wanted to get away from the war in their country.

William the Conqueror arrives in England

English people

Today, nearly fifty million people live in England, and thousands more come and live here every year. They come from Eastern Europe, from Afghanistan, Pakistan, and Iraq, from Australia, Canada and India, and many other countries. Some are looking for work; some want to be with their families; others are looking for a better life. They bring with them their theatre, food, music, and art.

Yes, you can find people from every part of the world here. So – what is England?

Come and see . . .

3   The big cities

London has more than eleven million visitors every year. They come and visit some of the most famous buildings in England: the Tower of London, St Paul's Cathedral, Westminster Abbey, and the Houses of Parliament.

Buckingham Palace is the Queen's London home. When she is staying at the palace, you can see her flag – the Royal Standard – at the front of the building. You can visit some of the rooms in August and September. Visitors like to take photos of the palace and of the soldiers outside.

London is full of museums and art galleries, theatres, and clubs. You can see and do lots of things here. For more about the city, read *London* (Oxford Bookworms Stage 1, Factfiles).

Soldiers outside Buckingham Palace

Birmingham is England's biggest city after London. In the year 1086, there were just twenty-five people in Birmingham, but now there are more than a million. Hundreds of years ago, people came to Birmingham's big market. Later they came for work; Birmingham was called 'the workplace of the world'. People made everything here, from cars to chocolate. Now it is famous for music, art, and shopping.

It is the home of the City of Birmingham Symphony Orchestra. You can hear them at Symphony Hall in Broad Street. Or you can listen to rock music from some of the UK's best bands at the Birmingham Academy in Dale End.

Birmingham Museum and Art Gallery in Chamberlain Square is one of the best galleries outside of London, with many wonderful paintings. At the Thinktank museum, you can learn about Birmingham's past, present, and future. There is also the National Sea Life Centre and the Birmingham Railway Museum.

A singer at Symphony Hall

For shopping, go to the Bullring. There are more than 160 shops in this big shopping mall, and you can see Selfridges' amazing building here. There are a lot of good places for food in the city, and many are not expensive. Go to the Chinese Quarter, near New Street Station, for the best Chinese restaurants.

Liverpool stands by the River Mersey on the north-west coast of England. It was the home of the Beatles in the 1960s, and many visitors go to the Beatles Story exhibition, or take a Beatles Tour. But it is also the home of the Grand National – one of England's most famous and important horse races – and two famous football clubs, Liverpool and Everton.

Horses in the Grand National

Albert Dock

Albert Dock has shops, restaurants, bars, museums, and art galleries. The first docks in Liverpool opened in 1715. Between 1830 and 1930, nine million people from all across Europe left Liverpool for a new life in America, Australia, Canada, or New Zealand. The Merseyside Maritime Museum tells the story of those interesting days in Liverpool.

There are lots of tours of the city by bus and on foot. You can take a boat across the Mersey for good views of the city and the docks. Another boat takes visitors up and down the River Mersey.

The Liverpool Empire is the city's biggest theatre. Or you can go to the Philharmonic Hall in Hope Street and hear the Royal Liverpool Philharmonic Orchestra. For rock and pop music, go to the Liverpool Academy at the University of Liverpool, or to the Cavern Club – famous because of the Beatles – in Mathew Street.

Visit Liverpool Cathedral at St James Mount; it is the fifth largest cathedral in the world. Or you can go to Tate Liverpool at Albert Dock. It has one of the best exhibitions of twentieth century art outside of London.

Manchester has one of the most famous football clubs in the world – Manchester United. It also has Europe's biggest shopping mall – the Trafford Centre. This has 280 shops, lots of cafés and restaurants, and a big cinema. You can drive there or go by bus from the city centre.

For small shops and pubs, visit the Northern Quarter. Afflecks Palace has more than fifty interesting shops in one building. King Street and Bridge Street have lots of clothes shops.

The Trafford Centre

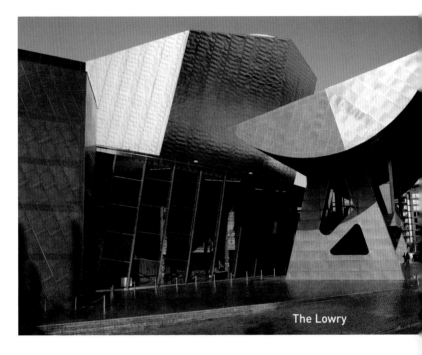

The Lowry

The city has many interesting museums. At the People's History Museum, at The Pump House in Bridge Street, you can learn about the lives of working people over the last 200 years. The Lowry, at Pier 8, Salford Quays, is a wonderful new building, with theatres and art galleries, and pictures by the Manchester artist L. S. Lowry. Lowry lived here from 1887 to 1976, and he painted the people and places around him – people at work, people in the streets, at football games, places in the city and in the country. Many people love his paintings.

The Royal Exchange Theatre is in St Ann's Square. Here you can see plays by some of today's best and most interesting writers. Or for an evening of laughs, visit The Comedy Store at Deansgate Locks.

4 More cities of England

Go north or south, east or west – other interesting cities are waiting for you.

Newcastle-upon-Tyne is on the north-east coast of England. Take a tour bus or a tour on foot and see the best of the city.

The Quayside – the part of the city near the river – has many cafés, bars, and restaurants. There are seven bridges across the River Tyne in the city, and the newest is the Gateshead Millennium Bridge. When big boats go up the river, the bridge can open and close, like an eye. You can walk across it to Gateshead Quays.

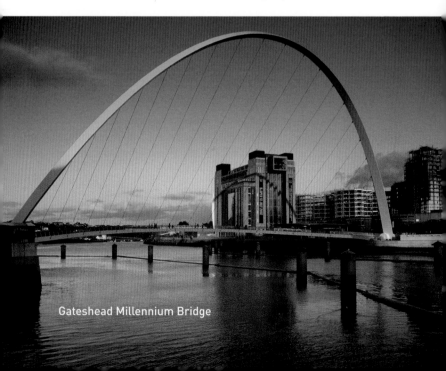

Gateshead Millennium Bridge

York

The Theatre Royal in Grey Street is one of England's most beautiful theatres. Or perhaps you go to the theatre because you like to laugh. Then the Hyena Café in Leazes Lane is the place for you. It opens on Thursday, Friday, and Saturday evenings.

In 1998 the Angel of the North arrived on a hill 7 kilometres from Newcastle. Some people like it, and some do not, but nearly every visitor to the north of England sees it. It is 20 metres high and 54 metres across, and you can take a bus to it from the city centre.

To the south of Newcastle, the city of York has some wonderful old buildings, castles, and museums. The city has a beautiful cathedral – York Minster – with amazing windows. And there are lots of great walks in York. You can take a walk along the river, through Roman York, or along the old city walls. And you can walk around the Liberty of St Peter – an old city inside the city of York.

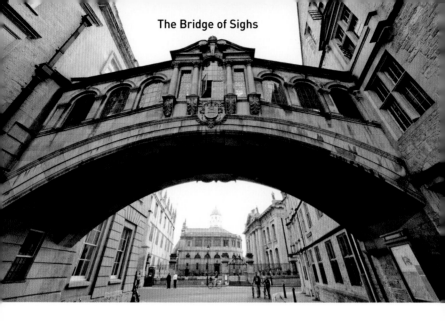

The Bridge of Sighs

Oxford and Cambridge are England's two most famous university cities. They are cities with rivers – Oxford has the Isis (the name for that part of the River Thames), and Cambridge has the Cam. You can see the city from a tour bus, or take a tour on foot. Or you can go in a flat boat called a punt and see the city from the river. After that, you can visit one of the many pubs and cafés, or look in a bookshop.

Oxford is near the centre of England. The Ashmolean Museum is one of the best museums in England. And Oxford's beautiful Bridge of Sighs is like the bridge with the same name in Venice.

When your feet are tired, go to the Oxford Story in Broad Street. A little train takes you past the story of the city. Or you can visit many of the thirty-nine colleges of the university. Look outside the colleges for visiting times – usually in the afternoons.

Cambridge is in the east of England, north of London. Cambridge University has thirty-one colleges, all in the centre of the city. King's College is one of the city's most beautiful buildings, and the singers from King's College are famous all over the world.

Many people like to visit the parks and college gardens next to the river. These are called the Backs. Here you can walk, or sit and read, or watch the punts on the river.

The city of Bath sits between green hills in the south-west of England. The city is famous for its Royal Crescent and other buildings.

Hot water comes out of the ground here, and the Romans built a city with baths. In the nineteenth century rich people came to Bath in their thousands. They listened to music, met and talked, and looked for a husband or a wife.

Today you can visit the Roman Baths. You can also go to the Assembly Rooms in Bennett Street. Rich visitors came to this beautiful building in the nineteenth century, and today it has the Museum of Costume, with clothes from the sixteenth century to today.

The Roman Baths in Bath

Clifton Suspension Bridge

There are many restaurants and cafés. Take tea in the Pump Rooms, or sit in the beautiful Parade Gardens.

Jane Austen, the writer of *Pride and Prejudice*, lived in Bath between 1801 and 1806. Visit the Jane Austen Centre in Gay Street and learn more about her and her books.

The city of Bristol is on the River Avon. Once boats from all over the world came up and down the river, but now the old docks are full of shops, cafés, and art galleries. England's oldest theatre, the Theatre Royal, is in Bristol. It was built in 1766.

Two interesting museums are the Bristol Industrial Museum at Prince's Wharf, and the City Museum and Art Gallery in Queen's Road. To the west of the city is the amazing Clifton Suspension Bridge, high above the River Avon. It was built in 1864.

When you visit towns and cities in England, you can use buses and taxis, and in London and Newcastle there are underground trains. But you see most when you walk – and it's free.

5   The coasts and countryside

You are never far from the sea in England. And you are never very far from some of the most beautiful countryside in the world. People say, 'It always rains in England.' Not true! But because it rains, the countryside is green and beautiful.

The Lake District National Park is in Cumbria, in the north-west of England. Here the hills are the highest in

A lake in the Lake District

England, and between them sit sixteen great lakes. Some – Buttermere, Wast Water – are quiet. Some – Windermere, Derwentwater – have towns beside the lakes and lots of boats. The Lake District is also a good place for walks, but be careful – the weather can change quickly.

The writer William Wordsworth lived in the Lake District. You can visit his home, Dove Cottage, at Grasmere. Another writer, Beatrix Potter, came to the Lake District in 1906 and lived here for many years. Children (and older people too) love her books about Peter Rabbit and other little animals.

On the wonderful long beaches of Northumbria, in the north-east of England, you can go for walks, watch birds, and get good views of some of Northumbria's castles. Alnwick Castle was 'Hogwarts School' in the Harry Potter films.

A beach in Northumbria

A green dale in Yorkshire

Yorkshire has two wonderful national parks. In the north-west is the Yorkshire Dales National Park. The three biggest dales – the places down between the hills – are Swaledale, Wharfedale and Wensleydale. There are hundreds of square kilometres of hills and dales, with fast rivers and nice little villages. There are castles at Richmond, Skipton, Middleham, and Castle Bolton, and a Countryside Museum at Hawes.

In the north-east is the North York Moors National Park. You can ride on the North Yorkshire Moors Railway or drive through beautiful countryside to Whitby or Robin Hood's Bay on the coast.

A boat on the Norfolk Broads

Three famous sisters lived at Haworth, in Yorkshire – the writers Charlotte, Emily, and Anne Brontë. Charlotte wrote *Jane Eyre*, Emily wrote *Wuthering Heights*, and Anne wrote *Agnes Grey*. You can visit the Brontë Parsonage Museum in Haworth. This little house was their home from 1820 to 1855.

In the Norfolk Broads, in the east of England, there is water everywhere, and no hills. You can go through the countryside by boat, or take one into the centre of Norwich, the biggest city in Norfolk. In the centre of this beautiful old city you can visit the castle and the eleventh century cathedral.

Dorset has wonderful walks along the south-west coast. See the amazing Chesil Bank beach, 13 kilometres long, near Abbotsbury, or visit Corfe Castle.

More than six million people come to the New Forest, in Hampshire, every year. Many come because they want to see the New Forest ponies. About 3,000 of these small horses live here. Other visitors like to walk in the forest or visit the little towns of Lyndhurst and Lymington.

In the south-west of England is Dartmoor National Park. There are ponies here too and it is a good place for long walks. You can read about Dartmoor in the famous Sherlock Holmes story, *The Hound of the Baskervilles* (Oxford Bookworms Stage 4).

Cornwall, in the far south-west, has great surfing beaches and wonderful walks on the coast. Many people like swimming, surfing, and visiting the beaches of the north coast around Newquay.

New Forest ponies

6 Days out

There are lots of big, beautiful old country houses – also called 'stately homes' – in England. Many of them are open to visitors, and you can go inside and see their wonderful rooms and beautiful paintings. In some country houses, the family live in part of the house.

One of the best is Castle Howard in Yorkshire. It has a beautiful house, and a big garden with two lakes. Another is Blenheim Palace near Oxford. Longleat in Wiltshire has a safari park, and you can watch the animals from your car. Woburn Abbey in Bedfordshire also has a safari park, and the house has paintings by Canaletto and Joshua Reynolds. At Beaulieu, in Hampshire, you can visit a museum of beautiful old cars, and you can also

Blenheim Palace

see the boats from the James Bond films. You can walk along the high walls of Warwick Castle in Warwickshire. And in Brighton, Sussex, you can visit the Royal Pavilion. King George the Fourth liked to come here in the early nineteenth century. The Pavilion is full of colour, with beautiful paintings on the walls.

You can walk to St Michael's Mount in Cornwall when the sea goes out. At other times you can take a boat from the little village of Marazion. When you get there, you can go up the hill and visit the old castle and church.

The Royal Pavilion

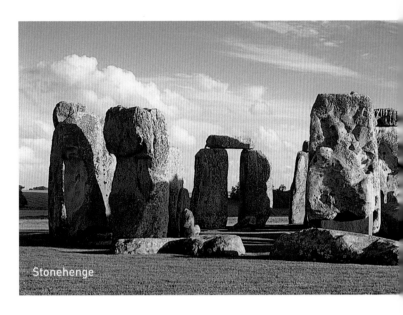

Stonehenge

Stonehenge, on Salisbury Plain in Wiltshire, was built between 3000 and 1500 BC. What is it for? Nobody knows. But every year thousands of people visit the stones. The tallest stones are nearly 7 metres high and some of them come from 250 kilometres away in Wales.

The Eden Project in Cornwall tells the story of hundreds of different plants. It has two 'biomes'. These are homes for plants from many places across the world – the USA, West Africa, South Africa, Malaysia, and South America. Outside the biomes there are thousands more plants, trees, and flowers. In the summer there are sometimes concerts in the evening.

Two more places with beautiful plants, trees, and flowers are the Royal Botanic Gardens at Kew, not far from London, and the Royal Horticultural Society gardens at Wisley in Surrey.

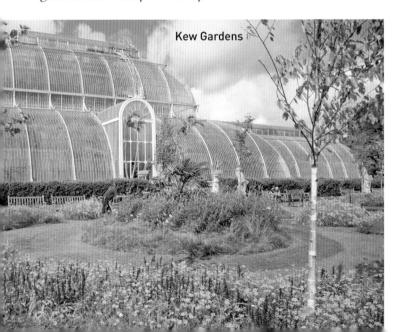

Kew Gardens

Alton Towers

You can visit the houses of some of the most famous English men and women. Jane Austen's house is at Chawton, near Winchester in Hampshire. She lived here for eight years and wrote *Mansfield Park*, *Emma*, and *Persuasion* here. Chartwell, near Sevenoaks in Kent, was the home of Sir Winston Churchill, Britain's Prime Minister at the time of the Second World War. He lived here for forty years. Or you can take a trip to the Isle of Wight (off the Hampshire coast) and visit Osborne House. This was one of the homes of Queen Victoria, Queen of England from 1837 to 1901.

Perhaps you like to have an exciting time when you go out. Then a theme park is for you. Go to Alton Towers in Staffordshire, or to Thorpe Park or Chessington World of Adventures in Surrey in the south of England.

7   Nights out

London's West End is famous for its theatres. There are more than fifty of them. But tickets can be expensive. Go in the afternoon – it's cheaper then.

Most of England's big cities, and many large towns, have theatres. Sometimes you can see plays at these theatres before they go to London's West End.

The Minack Theatre, Porthcurno, Cornwall, is different from other theatres – it is outside. You can see plays here in the summer.

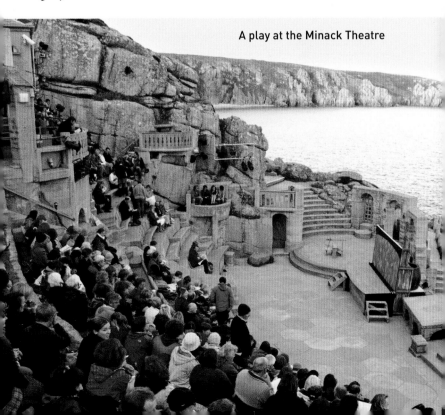

A play at the Minack Theatre

England's most famous writer is William Shakespeare. He was born in Stratford-upon-Avon and you can see his plays there at the Royal Shakespeare Theatre, next to the River Avon. Before you leave the town, you can visit Shakespeare's house. Many people also like to visit the home of Shakespeare's wife, Anne Hathaway, with its beautiful garden. It is north-west of the town in the little village of Shottery.

In the big cities there are lots of concerts. London, Birmingham, Bournemouth, Manchester, and Liverpool all have world-famous orchestras. The church of St Martin's in the Fields in Trafalgar Square in London has concerts at lunchtime on some days of the week. Cathedrals and churches in many other towns and cities have concerts too.

But you can listen to music in other places too – theatres, pubs, town centres and shopping malls. And you can dance and listen to music in clubs in most cities and large towns. Sometimes you need to get tickets, so get there early.

The Glastonbury Festival, at Pilton near Glastonbury in Somerset, is England's biggest rock music festival. It is usually on the last weekend in June. You can see and hear some of the best bands in the country, but you must buy your ticket in February. Other music festivals are at Leeds, Reading, Guildford, Chelmsford, and the Isle of Wight.

The Glastonbury Festival

8 From football to tennis

There are football clubs all over England. The biggest clubs are in cities – London, Manchester, Liverpool, Newcastle, Sheffield, and Birmingham. The big London clubs are Arsenal, Tottenham Hotspur, Chelsea, Fulham, West Ham United, and Charlton Athletic. But most towns have a football club. Games are on Saturday and Sunday afternoons, and some evenings, from August to May.

Rugby is a fast and exciting game. Most towns and cities have rugby clubs. In December you can see the big game between Oxford and Cambridge Universities at Twickenham, London.

Rugby

Cricket

The game of cricket began in England. Many people love to watch it in villages on Saturday and Sunday afternoons. You can see cricket from April to September. Go to Lords Cricket Ground in St John's Wood, London, or one of the great cricket clubs in Yorkshire, Lancashire, or Surrey.

For runners, two important races are the London Marathon in April and the Great North Run in June. The London Marathon goes through the streets of the city, from Greenwich to Westminster. The Great North Run is 21 kilometres long, and 50,000 people run in it each year. It starts in the centre of Newcastle and finishes in South Shields.

The Isle of Man, off the west coast of England, has famous motorcycle races every year, for two weeks at the end of May and the beginning of June.

Every year at the end of June, you can watch the Wimbledon Lawn Tennis Championships, in Wimbledon, south-west London. Famous tennis players come from all over the world.

9 English food

Why not start the day with the great English breakfast? Egg, bacon, sausages, tomatoes, mushrooms, and baked beans, with lots of tea. You can get an English breakfast at nearly all hotels, and at many cafés. When you have an English breakfast in the morning, you do not need to eat much for lunch.

An English pub is a good place for lunch and a drink. You can get hot or cold food, and it is not expensive. Other places for lunch are sandwich shops and coffee shops. There are also places with food and drink in shopping malls.

An English breakfast

Afternoon tea

The English like 'afternoon tea'. With your cup of tea you get sandwiches and cakes. You can get this at many hotels and restaurants, and there are tea shops in towns all across England.

For dinner, you can choose from restaurants with food from nearly every country in the world. You can go to a very comfortable, expensive restaurant, or for cheaper food, look for a pizzeria, or for English fish and chips. And there are lots of Indian restaurants in England – food is often cheap and good there.

Lancashire hotpot

When you move around England, ask about the food in different parts of the country. In Kent there are wonderful apples, and Cheddar in Somerset is famous for its cheese. Markets are good places for things like these.

Fish and chips

10 Clothes and shopping

London is the place for fashion in England. Mary Quant made the first miniskirt here in the 1960s. She was soon famous all round the world. Later, in the 1970s, Vivienne Westwood opened her shop Seditionaries in the King's Road in Chelsea, and punk fashion was born.

Punk fashion

London Fashion Week

Now, in February and September every year, there is London Fashion Week. People from many countries come and see clothes by Paul Smith, Bruce Oldfield, Katharine Hamnett and others. You can also go to shops in Sloane Street, New Bond Street, and Old Bond Street for fashion clothes.

One of England's most famous shops is Harrods, in Knightsbridge in London. It has nearly everything!

You can find many of the other big shops in out-of-town shopping malls, cities, and towns all over the country. For clothes, go to Marks and Spencer, Top Shop, River Island, and Monsoon. Waterstones and Borders have books, and HMV and Virgin have CDs and DVDs.

But don't forget the small shops. Here you can often find something different or more interesting. Most museums and galleries also have gift shops.

Many English towns have markets. Here you can find food, clothes, hats, bags, books, and other interesting things, and often they are not expensive.

You can find the cheapest food in the big supermarkets – Tesco, Sainsbury's, Asda, Morrisons, and Waitrose. But go to the smaller shops, markets and farm shops for something different.

Small shops in Brighton

11   All the year round

Interesting things are happening all the year round all over England.

In March or April you can watch the Oxford and Cambridge University Boat Race between Putney and Mortlake in London. Thousands of people come down to the river and watch the two boats.

Also in March or April is the Grand National – a long and exciting horse race at Aintree, Liverpool. Many of the horses never finish the race, but the first horse gets more than a million euros.

In May there is the Chelsea Flower Show at the Royal Hospital, in London. Here you can see the most beautiful flowers and gardens.

The Oxford and Cambridge Boat Race

Notting Hill Carnival

At the Henley Royal Regatta, at the end of June and the beginning of July, you can see boat races on the River Thames.

At the Royal Show in Kenilworth, Warwickshire, you can see the best of the countryside, with beautiful animals and great food. It is in July every year.

More than two million visitors watch the Notting Hill Carnival in London, on the last Sunday and Monday in August. There are two exciting parades with lots of music and noise, one on Sunday, and one on Monday. You can hear seventy or more bands, and watch 7,500 people in the parades. They go through the streets near Ladbroke Grove and Kensal Road.

Cowes

Cowes, on the Isle of Wight, has a festival of boat races every August. More than 8,000 people come to Cowes for the races in the waters around the island.

In October, you can see some of the best horses in the country at the Horse of the Year Show at the National Exhibition Centre in Birmingham.

Some towns and cities have summer festivals. You can listen to writers when they talk about their books. You can watch plays or dancing, listen to music, watch street theatre or a parade. Brighton (in May), Bath (in June), Aldeburgh in Suffolk (in June), and Cambridge (in July) are only four of the many places with festivals each year.

England has so many different things. You can't see everything in one visit, but you can come back again . . . and again . . . and again. England is always ready to say, 'Hello! Nice to see you!'

GLOSSARY

amazing very interesting and different

art pictures and other beautiful things that people like to look at

band a number of people who make music together

beach the place where you can walk next to the sea

boat a small ship for travelling on water

bus a kind of big 'car' which many people can travel in

cake a sweet food made with flour, butter and sugar

castle a large, stone building

century a time of 100 years

cheese yellow or white food made from milk

church a building where people pray to God

clothes things you wear, e.g. shirts, trousers, dresses

club a place where you go to dance and listen to music

coast the part of the land that is near the sea

college a part of a university

countryside land with trees, rivers etc. that is away from towns

dance to move your body to music

exhibition a number of things people go to look at e.g. in a museum or gallery

fashion new styles of clothes that a lot of people like and want to wear

festival a time when a lot of people come together to have fun, make music, dance etc.

flag a piece of cloth with a special pattern on it; every country has its flag

food what you eat

gallery a place where you can see paintings and other kinds of art

king the most important man in a country

life the time that you are alive

market a place where people go to buy and sell things; often outside

moor wild land on hills, with grass but not many trees

motorcycle a large bicycle with an engine

museum a place where you can look at old or interesting things

music when you sing or play an instrument, you make music

painting a picture made with paint

park a large place with trees and gardens where people can go to walk, play games etc.

plant something that grows in the ground

play (n) you go to the theatre to see a play

pony a small horse

pub a place where people go to have a drink, meet friends, etc.

queen the most important woman in a country

restaurant a place where people can buy and eat meals

safari park a park where you can see big wild animals – lions, monkeys etc

shopping mall a large building with many shops inside it

show a group of things in one place that people go to see

saint (St) part of the name of a very good or holy person; often written as St

story words that tell you about what happened in a certain place or time

theatre a building where you go to see plays

tour a short visit to see a building or city

university a place where people go to study after they leave school

view what you can see from a certain place

wall a side of a building or a room

war fighting between countries or groups of people

England

ACTIVITIES

ACTIVITIES

Before Reading

1 Match the words to the pictures.

1 ☐ food   3 ☐ boat   5 ☐ beach
2 ☐ cricket   4 ☐ castle   6 ☐ play

ACTIVITIES

While Reading

Read Chapters 1, 2, 3, and 4. Here are some untrue sentences about them. Change them into true sentences.

1 The Romans lived in England for about one hundred years.
2 The Vikings came to England from America.
3 Many German people came to England with William of Normandy.
4 Today, nearly ninety million people live in England.
5 Blenheim Palace is the Queen's home in London.
6 Liverpool is England's biggest city after London.
7 Manchester stands by the River Mersey on the north-west coast of England.
8 L. S. Lowry painted the people and places of Newcastle.
9 Newcastle has three bridges across the River Tyne.
10 Oxford and Cambridge have famous airports.
11 In the Assembly Rooms in Bath you can see books from the sixteenth century to today.
12 The oldest theatre in England is the Theatre Royal in London.

Read Chapters 5 and 6. Complete the sentences with the names of the places.

1 Beatrix Potter and William Wordsworth lived in the

   _____.

2 You can visit the house of three famous sisters in

   _____ in Yorkshire.

3 The biggest city in Norfolk is _____.

4 _____ in Wiltshire has a safari park.

5 King George the Fourth liked to visit _____.

6 _____ is a very old place on Salisbury Plain.

7 The _____ Project, in Cornwall, tells the story of

   plants.

8 _____, in Staffordshire, is a theme park.

Read Chapters 7 and 8. Are these sentences true or false? Change the false sentences into true ones.

1 London's West End is famous for its theme parks.

2 England's most famous singer is William Shakespeare.

3 Glastonbury has England's biggest rock music festival.

4 Football clubs play games from May to December.

5 Many people love to watch cricket in villages.

6 The Great North Run starts in York.

7 The Isle of Man has famous horse races every year.

8 Tennis players come from all over the world to play at

   Wimbledon.

Read Chapters 9 and 10. Match the beginnings and the endings of the sentences.

1 English pubs are a good place for …
2 For afternoon tea you get a cup of tea and …
3 There are tea shops in towns…
4 Cheddar in Somerset is famous for…
5 One of England's most famous shops is…
6 You can find the cheapest food in …

a the big supermarkets.
b sandwiches and cakes.
c all across England.
d lunch and a drink.
e its cheese.
f Harrods, in Knightsbridge.

Read Chapter 11. Match the shows and races with the things you can see there.

1 Grand National   a bands
2 Chelsea   b boats
3 Henley Royal Regatta   c animals
4 Royal Show   d flowers
5 Notting Hill Carnival e horses

ACTIVITIES

After Reading

1 Pierre is visiting England. Here are three of his postcards. Match the postcards (a, b, or c) to the words. Where did he get each postcard?

1 I went on a tour of this lake by boat. The water was very cold, but the countryside was beautiful. Later I went for a walk across the hills with some friends. We had a good view of the lakes.

Postcard _____ Place _____

2 After a long walk on the coast, I came to this beach. There were lots of people in the sea. The next day I tried surfing too – it was great!

Postcard _____ Place _____

3 Do you like this building? I saw it today and it's called The Lowry building. L. S. Lowry did lots of interesting paintings of the people of this northern city. I really liked the building too – it's very new.

Postcard _____ Place _____

a

b

c

2 Use the clues below to complete this crossword with words
   from the story. Then find the hidden ten-letter place name
   in the crossword.

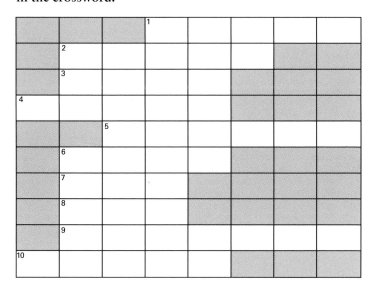

1 You make _____ when you sing.
2 Where you can walk next to the sea.
3 The Beatles were a famous _____.
4 To move your body to music.
5 A building where people pray to God.
6 What you can see from a certain place.
7 A big 'car' that a lot of people can travel in.
8 Pictures and other beautiful things.
9 You go to a _____ to see plays.
10 Words that tell you about what happened at a certain
   place or time.

The hidden place name in the crossword is _____.

‚ **Your friend Maria is in England. Read her e-mail and circle the correct words.**

From: Maria
Subject: England

Hi!

Today/Yesterday I am in Stratford-upon-Avon.
Tonight/Last night I am going to *look at/see* a *film/play* by *William Shakespeare/Anne Hathaway* at the Royal Shakespeare Theatre. Before that I am going to *visit/buy* the *house/theatre* of Shakespeare's *wife/daughter* Anne Hathaway. It has a very nice *park/garden.*

On Sunday I am going by train to Oxford in the *north/centre* of England. I want to visit the famous *Ashmolean/Bridge of Sighs* Museum. It is one of the best in *England/Scotland.*

Love, Maria

4 **Choose a place in England and write an e-mail about it.**

Dear _____,

Today I'm in ____. This morning I went to _____. This afternoon I'm going to _____ and later I want to visit _____. Tonight I want to see _____. Tomorrow I'm going by _____ to _____ in the _____ of England. When I get there I want to visit _____.

I'm coming home on _____.

See you soon!

ABOUT THE AUTHOR

John Escott worked in business before becoming a writer. Since then he has written many books for readers of all ages. He was born in Somerset, in the west of England, but now lives in Bournemouth in the south. From here he can easily reach the Dorset coast, which, he says, is his favourite part of England. When he is not working, he likes looking for long-forgotten books in small backstreet bookshops, watching old Hollywood films, and walking for miles along empty beaches.

He has visited many different places in England, and his favourite city is Bath, because of its fine buildings and its beautiful location. Among his other favourite English things are roast beef and Yorkshire pudding, English breakfasts, and the story of Robin Hood.

He has written or retold more than twenty stories for Oxford Bookworms, from Starter to Stage 6, and he has also written for the Oxford Dominoes series. His other Oxford Bookworms titles at Stage 1 are *New York* and *London* (Factfiles), *Goodbye, Mr Hollywood* (Thriller and Adventure), and *Sister Love and Other Crime Stories* (Crime and Mystery).

OXFORD BOOKWORMS LIBRARY

Classics • Crime & Mystery • Factfiles • Fantasy & Horror
Human Interest • Playscripts • Thriller & Adventure
True Stories • World Stories

The OXFORD BOOKWORMS LIBRARY provides enjoyable reading in English, with a wide range of classic and modern fiction, non-fiction, and plays. It includes original and adapted texts in seven carefully graded language stages, which take learners from beginner to advanced level. An overview is given on the next pages.

All Stage 1 titles are available as audio recordings, as well as over eighty other titles from Starter to Stage 6. All Starters and many titles at Stages 1 to 4 are specially recommended for younger learners. Every Bookworm is illustrated, and Starters and Factfiles have full-colour illustrations.

The OXFORD BOOKWORMS LIBRARY also offers extensive support. Each book contains an introduction to the story, notes about the author, a glossary, and activities. Additional resources include tests and worksheets, and answers for these and for the activities in the books. There is advice on running a class library, using audio recordings, and the many ways of using Oxford Bookworms in reading programmes. Resource materials are available on the website <www.oup.com/elt/gradedreaders>.

The *Oxford Bookworms Collection* is a series for advanced learners. It consists of volumes of short stories by well-known authors, both classic and modern. Texts are not abridged or adapted in any way, but carefully selected to be accessible to the advanced student.

You can find details and a full list of titles in the *Oxford Bookworms Library Catalogue* and *Oxford English Language Teaching Catalogues*, and on the website <www.oup.com/elt/gradedreaders.

THE OXFORD BOOKWORMS LIBRARY
GRADING AND SAMPLE EXTRACTS

STARTER • 250 HEADWORDS

present simple – present continuous – imperative –
can/cannot, must – *going to* (future) – simple gerunds ...

Her phone is ringing – but where is it?

Sally gets out of bed and looks in her bag. No phone. She looks under the bed. No phone. Then she looks behind the door. There is her phone. Sally picks up her phone and answers it. *Sally's Phone*

STAGE 1 • 400 HEADWORDS

... past simple – coordination with *and*, *but*, *or* – subordination with *before, after, when, because, so* ...

I knew him in Persia. He was a famous builder and I worked with him there. For a time I was his friend, but not for long. When he came to Paris, I came after him – I wanted to watch him. He was a very clever, very dangerous man. *The Phantom of the Opera*

STAGE 2 • 700 HEADWORDS

... present perfect – *will* (future) – *(don't) have to, must not, could* – comparison of adjectives – simple *if* clauses – past continuous – tag questions – *ask/tell* + infinitive ...

While I was writing these words in my diary, I decided what to do. I must try to escape. I shall try to get down the wall outside. The window is high above the ground, but I have to try. I shall take some of the gold with me – if I escape, perhaps it will be helpful later. *Dracula*